— DR. MIKEL A. BROWN —

HEALTHY
GOD WANTS YOU
WEALTHY &
FULL OF LIFE

POWER UP YOUR LIFE BY LEARNING HOW TO LIVE HEALTHIER, BUILD WEALTH, AND ENJOY LIFE TO THE FULLEST.

" EVERY SERIOUS STUDENT OF UNCOMMON WISDOM WILL FIND HIS BOOK A TRUE GOLDMINE."

– DR. MIKE MURDOCK

CJ PUBLISHING COMPANY

EL PASO, TEXAS

God Wants You Healthy, Wealthy, and Full of Life

PUBLISHING COMPANY

1208 Sumac Drive
El Paso, TX 79925

Copyright © 2005 by Mikel Brown
Printed in the United States of America
Library of Congress Control Number: 2005926711
ISBN: 1-930388-09-8

Editorial assistance for CJC Publishing Co. by Gary Sparkman

Cover design by Charles Bennett III
Published by CJC Publishing Company

All scriptures are quoted from the King James Version, The New International Version, and the The Living Bible

---

All rights reserved. No portion of this book may be used without the written permission of the publisher, with the exception of brief excerpts in magazine articles, reviews, etc. For further information or permission, address CJC Publishing Co. 1208 Sumac Drive, El Paso, Texas 79925

Table of Contents

DEDICATION..V

PREFACE..VII

CHAPTER 1
The Principle of Being Healthy, Wealthy and Full of Life.......2

CHAPTER 2
You Were Born to Be Great 18

CHAPTER 3
The Dynamic Points of Optimism..24

CHAPTER 4
Projecting a Strong Self-Image...36

CHAPTER 5
Discovering the Wealth Within 44

CHAPTER 6
Mastering the Fundamentals of Success...................................54

CHAPTER 7
Reaching for the Top...58

CHAPTER 8
I Can... 62

PEARLS OF WISDOM 67

NOTES..74

ABOUT THE AUTHOR..77

IV

Dedication

To my lifelong friend and wife for her unselfish devotion to me and my calling. To my children Joshua, Mikayla, Mikelle, Marquita, and Mikel Jr. who are part of the generation to which I've dedicated my efforts: to the many people whose lives will be touched and forever changed after reading this book.

Special Thanks

My heartfelt thanks and deepest appreciation to the following spiritual sons and daughters, and friends whose financial seeds have enabled the consummation of this project. I Love You!

Savaslas & Tracey Lofton (Music in my ear)
Derrick & Varonica Jones
Alan & Alma Spence
Reggie & Nancy Mainor
Scott & Laura Whittle
Roy & Tish Times
Gregory & Monica Austin
Bryan & Tracie Reed
Jameelah Joshua
Willie & Katherine Jenkins
Bill & Becky Smith

Preface

A recent report was given concerning the mental health of the American public. Psychiatrists say that at least 50% of the American public has at one time or another been to a psychiatrist or is presently seeing one. People are generally unhappy with their lives and the outlook of their future. While people need to feel good about their life and hopeful concerning their future, the secrets to knowing how seems to elude most of us. *"God Wants You HEALTHY, WEALTHY, AND FULL OF LIFE"* is a complete guide to help people feel good, increase their income, and gives them the tools to believe that they deserve to be Healthy, Wealthy, and Full of Life. These special tips are a real confidence booster without the side-effects of being guilty about feeling so great about your life and where your life is headed. Dr. Mikel Brown shares the secrets to wealth and vitality. After reading his book entitled, *"Beyond Ordinary: Success is Only a Thought Away,"* I made the assumption that you can't get any better than this. Well, I was wrong! Dr. Brown pulled out nuggets that not only will make you believe that your life can be better, but why it will get better.

chapter one

The Principle of Being Healthy, Wealthy and Full of Life

chapter one 1

The Principle of Being Healthy, Wealthy and Full of Life

Psychiatrists say that most people are generally unhappy with their present state and are clueless to how to change it. Some people aren't happy because they believe that it is unrealistic to even conceive such a notion. They have the misconception that happiness is an illusion and that no one in their right mind can truly be happy. People have been subliminally taught that if one area of an individual's life is going well, other parts of their life must be suffering. This, my friend is absolutely absurd. You have an inalienable right to be happy and to live your dreams. You deserve all that earth has birthed for you. Unfortunately, you do not receive in this world what you deserve; you get what you take. And believe me, it is all for the taking. Dare to establish a healthy self-esteem and realize that your dreams are meant to come true.

I believe that I have a mandate on my life to help people get to the place where they can live out the rest of their days healthy, wealthy, and full of life. Success and happiness are by-products of living with fidelity to God and to self. They must never be viewed as goals we struggle to achieve.

> A lady, while her husband was absent, lost both her children to cholera. She laid them out with a mother's tenderness, spread a sheet over them, and waited at the door for her husband's return.
>
> "A person lent me some jewels," she told her husband on his return, "and he now wants to have them back. What shall I do?" "Return them, by all means," said the husband. Silently uncovering the lifeless bodies, she revealed to her husband the precious jewels of which she spoke.
>
> **1Cor 3:13 (TLB)** There is going to come a time of testing at Christ's Judgment Day to see what kind of material each builder has used. Everyone's work will be put through the fire so that all can see whether or not it keeps its value, and what was really accomplished.

I am concerned not only with how your life is going now, but also with how it ends up later. My fervent hope is that you would not simply settle for mediocrity but strive for excellence in every area of your life. My aim is not to get you to make a mere impression in life, but a strong impact. Allow me to help you build or rebuild your life with quality materials; you'll be glad you did. I would like to point out two things first.

1. What is the quality of the materials of which your life is made?

Quality can be best described as the true essence that defines and distinguishes a particular thing. In other words, it can be the grade, the degree of, or the classification by which you can properly assess or appraise the value of something. The quality of a product depends on the quality of the materials used to make it. Likewise, the quality of your life is determined by the quality of the materials you are using to build it. Your quality of life or station in life can be no greater than what you find yourself listening to, watching, pondering, and doing all day long.

> **Pearl of Wisdom**
>
> "When you relax the standard, you lessen the quality."

The old Zenith television commercial would end with this phrase: "The quality goes in before the name goes on." The more you build your life on truth, the better will be your way and the greater will be your life. Truth is like detergent—it's no good unless it's applied. The cheaper the merchandise, the higher the gloss (surface shine)! My friend, this is true of furniture, jewelry, marriages and people.

2. Is it easier to give an excuse for your failure or accept the responsibility for them?

The Principle of Being Healthy, Wealthy and Full of Life

Generally, people fail in life because they make half-hearted attempts at achieving their endeavors. People do the wrong thing because they've not been properly trained to do the right thing. And parents can be the biggest contributors to helping their children do wrong things because they do not teach them how to do what is right. When you relax the standard, you lessen the quality.

> "Ninety-nine percent of the failures come from people who have the habit of making excuses."
> – *George Washington Carver*

Excuses are tools of incompetence that lead people down a path of failure that they will eventually adapt to and embrace as part of their lifestyle. One of the most difficult things to accomplish is to rid people of toxic mentalities. How do you get individuals to change for the better when they have only known how to be the person they presently are? Children and adults alike are often told to change their lifestyles and behavior, but most have never been taught how to change them. Consistent mistakes are a result of a thinking pattern that locks the person into a non-productive routine. People who are accustomed to living on the lower rungs of life can only produce the environments with which their thought patterns are familiar. Many people have been told all their lives that the wealthy are special; that poor people have a better chance of getting into heaven; or that you should not want to be wealthy because it means that you will be selfish. If this is what individuals have been indoctrinated with all their lives, is there any

Pearl of Wisdom

"Excuses are tools of incompetence that lead people down a path of failure that they will eventually adapt to and embrace as part of their lifestyle."

Pearl of Wisdom

"People who have amassed great wealth believe they're entitled to it, while those without much wealth hold negative views of those who possess it."

wonder why many find it difficult to initiate the change that will improve their lives. They are only relating and living the life that they have been taught. Consequently, as they hear the phrase, "God wants you healthy, wealthy, and full of life" their present pattern of thinking will be antagonistic towards these words.

I have learned that it is not that people do not want to change; it is that they do not have a clue as to how to go about making the needed positive change. These people will have to go through a detoxification process because they are heavily influenced by previous negative thought patterns. What you have been taught all your life is usually what you believe and have set as a standard for living. If you break the previous warped thought pattern, but do not develop a healthier and more balanced one, you will simply regress back into your old, self-defeating pattern of behavior.

One of the most dangerous and damaging lies ever told to mankind is that God, who created mankind, heaven and earth, does not want His creation enjoying the wealth of planet earth. It is very difficult to comprehend just how damaging this lie has been. Millions of people are convinced of this lie without evidence to support their beliefs. There is no biblical basis to support their notions, only opinions rooted in personal lack and insufficiency. People who have amassed great wealth believe they're entitled to it, while those without much wealth hold negative views of those who possess it. One wealthy family was having dinner with a guest of their daughter when the subject of money came

The Principle of Being Healthy, Wealthy and Full of Life

up. The mother said to the guest, "We do not discuss money at the dinner table because money is not important to us." The guest simply looked at the mother enjoying her meal while calling for the black servant, and he became slightly irritated and replied, "Madam, your thinking that money is not important is simply predicated on the fact that you have it. But people, who don't have much of it, realize how important money really is."

> **Pearl of Wisdom**
>
> "What you believe about wealth and money is directly proportionate to how much of it you possess."

What you believe about wealth and money is directly proportionate to how much of it you possess. This is one reason why most people are frustrated with trying to get ahead financially. They soon discover that the harder they try to get ahead, the further behind they fall. Get your head out of box and think! The box is symbolic of prison, slavery, and/or small thinking. Step out into the open expanse and watch your creative juices begin to flow. If you choose to think inside the box, you are in no position to question your results. Favorable results are not the accident of an unpredictable God. God rewards the faith we employ, but resists blessing those who refuse to apply His laws of increase.

Let's examine your thoughts on prosperity and gauge what you truly believe. Okay, you concur that prosperity covers more than just financial increase, but in your heart of hearts, you may lean more towards the notion that money represents the greater part of what prosperity entails. A person once said, "I don't want to be wealthy or rich, I just want to live a comfortable lifestyle." I laugh at statements like this! What do you think wealth really is? It is having enough to live comfortably. If you can pay your bills, give ten percent of your income and offerings to your church, put away money every month in a savings account, and have more left over to help others in need, you are wealthy.

> **Pearl of Wisdom**
>
> "God is not the God of just enough; He is the God of more than enough."

Living comfortably does not consist entirely of just being able to pay one's bills. Living a comfortable lifestyle encompasses so much more. So, again! What are your true thoughts about wealth? What do you want to experience in your life? Whatever it is, God wants it a million times more than you do. And, what bad you don't want to happen in your life, God doesn't want you to experience it a million times more than your desire to avoid the unfortunate. Let's face it! God wants you healthy, wealthy, and full of the life of God.

Where do people start when their thoughts have been warped by erroneous teachings? Change what you have been taught about God's will for your life, and His word will reveal the necessary change you must embrace. Since change is inevitable, you might as well change for the better.

> **Jere 29:11 (NIV)** For I know the plans I have for you," declares the LORD, "plans to prosper you and not to harm you, plans to give you hope and a future.

If anyone has ever proven how much they love me, God has. He sent His only begotten Son to planet earth to die for my sins. I can't imagine God placing man in the Garden of Eden without sufficient resources to sustain him. It is actually a healthy God esteem to believe that God has your best interest at heart. God created everything in the Garden of Eden for Adam and Eve, and said, "Go for it." God is not the God of just enough; He is the God of more than enough. Why is it that people who lack much, usually complain that people with much have too much?

How much is too much? Is the answer to this question actually relative? When a wealthy person chooses to own ten different automobiles, do you consider that excessive? If a wealthy family chooses to live in a twenty-five thousand square foot home, is this too much space for a family of three? If you can honestly say that this is going overboard, then you may harbor resentment toward those who are wealthy, and your thinking is absolutely unhealthy. "But you can only drive one car at a time" you may say. But in truth, how many pairs of shoes can you wear at one time? Or how many clothing outfits can you put on at one time? Do you believe that owning more than one pair of shoes is excessive? There are people in third world nations who do not have one pair of shoes; however, your closet is full of shoes and clothes that you hardly wear. It is hypocritical of someone to criticize a person about being excessive when they too live extravagant lifestyles, albeit to a lesser degree. How can anyone conclude that his or her excess of shoes, clothes, and even food are any different than the plethora of automobiles someone else may own?

Pearl of Wisdom

"How much is too much?"

God wants you Healthy, Wealthy & Full of Life

Pearl of Wisdom

....

"The more you are exposed to truth, the clearer your directions will be in life."

....

Pearl of Wisdom

....

"Lack is not an option when abundance is a lifestyle."

....

Please allow me to continue before you weigh-in with your opinion. Don't put this book down yet! I'm not finished! If you give me a chance to elaborate further, I believe I can help you gain a proper perspective of God's will for you concerning wealth. Think of all the unnecessary items you presently have in your possession. I can give you a list of things without knowing you personally or ever having been to your home or business. How much food do you waste in a day? Have you ever thought about the restaurants that you dine in when you have food at home? You may not feel wealthy by America's standard, but people in third world countries would love to trade places with you at anytime.

In truth, we all live with a great deal of excesses in our lives. At this point, we are now simply talking about degrees of excessive living, but who is qualified to draw the line between whose excessive lifestyle is outrageous and whose is reasonably justified. The answer always lies within the heart of the one passing judgment. So before you make a judgment based upon someone else's wealth, read the following scriptures.

> **Matt 7:3 (NIV)** "Why do you look at the speck of sawdust in your brother's eye and pay no attention to the plank in your own eye?
> 4 How can you say to your brother, `Let me take the speck out of your eye,' when all the time there is a plank in your own eye?
> 5 You hypocrite, first take the plank out of

your own eye, and then you will see clearly to remove the speck from your brother's eye.

I removed the beam from my eye some fifteen years ago, which helped me to see clearly to remove toothpicks from the eyes of others. I do not claim to have cornered the market on wisdom governing financial matters- far be it from me to make such a claim. I simply want what is best for God's people. The more you are exposed to truth, the clearer your directions will be in life.

Abundance is our daily, allotted portion from God. Does abundance have limits? No!!! Abundance exceeds the "need" level and even extends deep into those dimensions of our lives where "wants" abide. In other words, lack is not an option when abundance is a lifestyle. God blessed Abraham, and he became rich. God blessed and he became very wealthy. God also blessed Abraham's grandson and God taught Jacob how to prosper. Beloved, I want you to believe that you are next in line. Change what you believe concerning God's desire for your wealth, and watch how your environment adapts to what you believe.

God Wants You Healthy

3 John 1:2 Dear friend, I pray that you may enjoy good health and that all may go well with you, even as your soul is getting along well. (NIV)

God wants you Healthy, Wealthy & Full of Life

Pearl of Wisdom

"A healthy person can enjoy his or her wealth."

A healthy person can enjoy his or her wealth. Is good health important to God? This is an age-old question that has been debated amongst bible critics throughout the ages critics who would have us believe that God's perfect will does not encompass good health or healing. The world is beginning to wake up to the importance of natural, organic foods. Processed foods are detrimental to the health of humans. Many human illnesses can be traced back to our eating habits. We have become addicted to fast foods, and we're turning into a society of junk food junkies. The majority of the American population is driven to satisfying its daily sugar addiction. Our physiological system is dependent upon these foods in order to feed the parasites that exist in most humans.

When my wife and I initially began our research on how to become healthier, I personally became baffled with all the conflicting information flooding our bookstores and internet search engines. In fact, much of it was down right frightening. I wanted to run straight to the local health food store and buy every natural, germ-fighting supplement I could find. I will not begin to count the cost of all the products I purchased. My wife became a health store fanatic, to say the least. We ordered every product from QVC, HSN, and Shop NBC. We spent a small fortune on products that we had read and heard about. Did these products help us? I know that they did not hurt us! The money was not the issue for me; for me, the issue was obtaining the right information to help me safeguard my health. I needed to make an

The Principle of Being Healthy, Wealthy and Full of Life

informed decision about my health and my conditioning, and I wanted to do it God's way.

My wife is a Registered Nurse by profession, and as such, she is naturally drawn to anything related to health and medicine. She is very knowledgeable of the many nuances of traditional medicine, but she was not versed in the area of natural wellness and holistic medicine. As she began her quest for understanding into the field of alternative medicine, I must say I was rather reluctant to join her on her journey. Needless to say, I accompanied her, and I am very glad I did.

There are many discoveries in the power of food to cure and prevent health problems. From aging and diabetes to ulcers and yeast infections, natural remedies have been uncovered in certain foods. These foods do not include processed foods which have only proven to act as a slow suicide attempt. Fruits and vegetables are the most neglected health remedies in the world. Pharmaceutical companies are craftily placing gag orders on doctors that can easily suggest natural foods to help their patients' ailing bodies. But if doctors direct people towards nature's remedies, the pharmaceutical companies will go out of business. Please don't get me wrong, I believe men have been endowed with certain abilities to discover remedies through man-made medicines, but after experiencing some of the side effects that may result from consuming these medicines, people will have to take other pills to help remedy what the first pills caused.

For instance: Corn is a natural crop that can help

> **Pearl of Wisdom**
>
> "When men have run out of options, God becomes the only option."

lower cholesterol and perhaps boost one's energy levels. But it can be a problem when the corn is processed. Many people are sensitive to processed corn—especially cereals made from corn which are among the top-five allergy causing foods. Grape Juice is a drink for the heart. Its healing power can lower cholesterol, decrease the risk of heart disease, and even lower high blood pressure. I am not the expert; I only read what researchers have unveiled. It's cheaper to buy fruits and vegetables to assist in aiding your medical condition than it is buying 30 pills for $200 that will most likely result in other medical conditions.

If God did not want people to be healthy, He would not have deposited the healing power in fruits and vegetables. Moreover, since our bodies come from the earth, our bodies are sustained by the products that this planet produces. It is a geographical reality that the earth is two-thirds water. And it is a biological fact that the human body is two-third water. It is a common and well documented fact that man, beast, and plants cannot live for any length of time without water. A person does not become dehydrated unless he or she was once hydrated. Consistently drinking water cut my migraine headaches by 99 percent. I used to experience at least 9 to 13 migraines a year. After I discovered the importance of 8 to 10 glasses of water a day, I inadvertently stumbled on how it reduced my migraines to 1 and sometimes zero migraines a year. When a person is hydrated, the water works like a lubrication which keeps most of your body parts running smoothly. So drink up!

The Principle of Being Healthy, Wealthy and Full of Life

Do I believe in divine healing? I'd better believe in it because despite the many precautions taken to avoid any sickness or injury, we cannot escape the air pollution that is causing humans serious health problems. When men have run out of options, God becomes the only option. Contrary to what many biblical scholars and seminary professors teach, healing is definitely a new testament, covenant entitlement that was made available as a result of the death and resurrection of Jesus Christ. Therefore, His will for you is that you live in the health that His dying secured. Many supposed experts put forth their opinions on this subject to the great detriment to their followers. Owing to the tremendous weight that science and medicine have in our society, it is little wonder why many find it difficult to accept the truth regarding divine healing today. When the latest, state-of-the-art medical technologies prove powerless to address your medical condition because your cancer has metastasized to the point where doctors have given up hope, then where do you turn for answers? While we are certain to experience sicknesses and diseases in this lifetime, God has provided a ready remedy for all those who would believe Him for their healing.

God wants you Healthy, Wealthy & Full of Life

chapter two

You Were Born To Be Great

chapter two

You Were Born To Be Great

People can do great things, but that does not make them great. Humans can get on their hands and knees and bark like a dog, but acting like a dog will not make them any more a dog than performing one great feat will make one great. There is a vast difference between being famous and being great. Achieving fame takes little effort; all that is needed is an audience of someone other than you. Fame can come simply by virtue of your being born to celebrity parents or to parents who have, themselves, done great things. People may become famous because of their talent or physical features. Greatness, however, comes as a result of fulfilling purpose and destiny. Fame comes from who you are, but greatness comes from whom you've helped. You can always follow the trail of people who are viewed to be great because they leave behind a legacy of people they have helped.

People with fame have a job to perform, but people with greatness have a calling to answer. When all you are interested in doing for the rest of your life is having an occupation and making money, you will

> **Pearl of Wisdom**
>
> "People with fame have a job to perform, but people with greatness have a calling to answer."

never qualify for greatness. It is not that you were not created to be great; it is simply that you may be unwilling to do great things. Great people experience no joy in occupying a job. Great people have a sense of urgency to answer their calling, which will result in their vocation.

Beginning something new might take you giving up something old. One of the greatest hindrances to your progression is chronically doing what doesn't work. If what you are doing did not work the last ten times you tried it, it usually will not work the following ten times. Repeating the same ineffective process will result in continuous failure. When people choose to remain married to ineffective methods, they will soon discover that their biggest barrier to progress will not be the obstacles in the path to their success but unjettisoned failed methodologies. Ignorance is this, in this regard will result in their undoing.

God has guaranteed your success in this life, and He only requires obedience on your part to inherit the success that is yours. Obedience to God will cause you to see what you could not have seen before. People usually cannot see their own greatness until they begin to obey God in doing what He called them to do. Moses would never have risen to the full stature of his greatness if he had not obeyed God's command to go back to Egypt. Gideon's contentment in the wheat field would have consumed his future had he not had an angel call him a mighty man of valor, thus elevating a lowly farmhand to a leadership position over the Army of Israel.

> **Pearl of Wisdom**
>
> "Intimidation is birthed out of the sphere of comparisons."

The greatness in a person emerges because of what he does, not because of who he is. If you desire to step into your greatness, you must be willing to do great things. Alexander was called the Great because of the many nations he conquered. Remember, no man becomes great sitting on his throne. Your season will change the moment you do what you were called to do.

Intimidation is a major problem with most people. Why is this, you might ask. What causes intimidation and how can a person overcome it? Intimidation is birthed out of the sphere of comparisons. People compare when they match their strength, weapons, talent, or other similar attributes against those of another, thus, creating either a false sense of confidence or a false sense of insecurity. If you learn to eliminate intimidation factors, you will endeavor to succeed with a greater resolve.

> **Pearl of Wisdom**
>
> "Mediocrity is the kryptonite to greatness."

It is very difficult to move people into an arena where they might have a glimpse of their greatness because they fear what might be waiting to oppose them there. Moreover, they have never envisioned themselves being great. Most people never aspire to become great because, in most cases, men and women are only interested in a standard of mediocrity. The words that people choose to believe about themselves will become the standard by which they live. Mediocrity is the kryptonite to greatness. There is no challenge in being mediocre. What do you say to a man who wants more, but settles for less? Nothing! If a man truly wants more out of life, he will take more out of it. But, if he is just talking with empty words, he will reason that what he has is enough.

People who settle for whatever comes their way in life are those who do not mind waiting under a tree for fruit to fall. They seldom object to stooping down to recover what lay on the ground beneath them. But people who have a flicker of greatness in them will never settle for simply waiting for fallen fruit. Their drive is for the best. Moreover, they are more apt to climb to the top of the tree where the fruit is oftentimes much better.

I have learned that God does not make people great; people cause people to become great. Those who achieve greatness earn such honor because they do what the majority of people are unwilling to do. The price for greatness can never be properly assessed and accounted for apart from strong opposition. For truly, it is the size of the opposition encountered that ascribes the proper weight of glory to those who wear the mantle of greatness. The price can only be calculated after we have withstood the opposition to do what is right. Rosa Parks started a civil rights bus boycott because she was tired of not standing for what was right. Because of her courage to defy the bigotry of her day, she became one of the most celebrated women of our time. Greatness does not make you perfect; it exposes your willingness to pursue it.

Responsibility for success depends on your willingness to be responsible for your failure. Most of our failure comes as a result of poor preparation. Failure to prepare is preparation for failure. Your

> **Pearl of Wisdom**
>
> "Greatness does not make you perfect; it exposes your willingness to pursue it."

> **Pearl of Wisdom**
>
> "There are winners and there are losers; and there are people who would like to think that they are somewhere in the middle."

test doesn't come while you're winning; your test comes after you lose. Why? Have you ever heard the winner whine? The one who says, "It's only a game." is usually the one losing. There are winners and there are losers; and there are people who would like to think that they are somewhere in the middle. To improve your quality of life, you must develop good habits that will increase your chances of making it in this world. Habits good or bad, are developed or broken by submission or resistance to instructions, preparation and training.

chapter three

The Dynamic Points Of Optimism

chapter three

The Dynamic Points of Optimism

We live in a society where most people are categorically opposed to people with a positive outlook on life. People who are optimistic about negative situations often aggravate those individuals who are pessimistic by nature. To dissuade you from achieving your goals, people with a negative view on life will first direct their attacks at the very object of your pursuits, telling you how pointless it is to desire such goals. Should their first attempts prove futile, they will then turn their venom against you as an individual.

Skeptics always believe that they have more going themselves than you have working for you. And despite your achievements, they will never allow themselves to see you any higher than they at their lowest point. This is one good reason why you should not waste your time trying to prove your critics wrong. If there is anybody who needs to be convinced about your ability to succeed—it is you! If you are convinced that what you have to offer the world is priceless, and you believe in yourself, why should you care about what others think? Your

Pearl of Wisdom

" If there is anybody who needs to be convinced about your ability to succeed—it is you!"

greatest victories in life will not come by simply overcoming the challenges posed by others; they will manifest after you have first conquered your own fears and insecurities.

Here is an interesting story that I think you will find amusing and noteworthy:

> A minister one-day discovered that his church was getting into serious financial troubles. Coincidentally, while checking the church storeroom, he discovered several cartons of new bibles that had never been opened and distributed. So at his Sunday sermon, he asked for three volunteers from the congregation who would be willing to sell the bibles door-to-door for $10 each to raise the desperately needed money for the church. **Peter, Paul and Louie** all raised their hands to volunteer for the task. The reverend knew that Peter and Paul earned their living as salesmen and that they would likely be capable of selling many of the bibles, but he had serious doubts about Louie. Louie was just a local farmer, who had always kept to himself because he was embarrassed about his speech impediment. Poor little Louis had a very bad stuttering problem. But, not wanting to discourage Louis, the reverend decided to let him try anyway.
>
> Anxious to find out how successful they

were, the reverend immediately asked Peter, "Well, Peter, how did you make out selling our bibles last week?" Proudly handing over the envelope he said, "Using my sales prowess, I was able to sell 20 bibles, and here's the $200 I collected on behalf of the church." "Fine job, Peter!" The reverend said, vigorously shaking his hand. "You are indeed a fine salesman and the Church is indebted to you."

Turning to Paul, he asked, "And Paul, how many bibles did you manage to sell for the church last week?" Paul, smiling and sticking out his chest, confidently replied, "Reverend, I am a professional salesman and was happy to give the church the benefit of my sales expertise. Last week I sold 28 bibles on behalf of the church, and here's $280." The reverend responded, "That's absolutely splendid, Paul. You are truly a professional salesman and the church is also indebted to you."

Apprehensively, the reverend turned to Louie and said, "And Louie, did you manage to sell any bibles last week?" Louie silently offered the reverend a large envelope. The reverend opened it and counted the contents. "What is this?" the reverend exclaimed. "Louie, there's $3200 in here! Are you suggesting that you sold 320 bibles for the church, door to door, in just one week? Louie just nodded.

The Dynamic Points of Optimism

"That's impossible!" both Peter and Paul said in unison. "We are professional salesmen, yet you claim to have sold 10 times as many bibles as we could." "Yes, this does seem unlikely," the reverend agreed. "I think you'd better explain how you managed to accomplish this, Louie."

Louie shrugged. "I-I-I- re-re-really do-do-don't kn-kn-know f-f-f-for sh-sh-sh-sure," he stammered. Impatiently, Peter interrupted. "For crying out loud, Louie, just tell us what you said to them when they answered the door!"

"A-a-a-all I-I-I s-s-said wa-wa-was," Louis replied, "W-w-would y-y-you l-l-l-like t-t-to b-b-b-buy th-th-this b-b-bible f-f-for t-t-ten b-b-b-bucks --o-or--- wo-wo-would yo-you j-j-j-just l-like m-m-me t-t-to st-st-stand h-h-here and r-r-read it t-to y-you?"

Jealous and negative people tend to suffer from strong insecurities and live secret lives of unhappiness. What is more disturbing is that they are often too afraid to deal with the source of their inner fears. They will often project their inner self-hatred outward onto others whom they deem to be more successful in given areas of life. For example, many overweight individuals harbor secret feelings of animosity against slender or more physically fit individuals because of an inner longing to be similarly proportioned. And here is where the

Pearl of Wisdom

"When we choose to use others as the yardstick to measure our success, we will always fall prey to destructive feelings of insecurity."

problem usually begins. When we choose to use others as the yardstick to measure our success, we will always fall prey to destructive feelings of insecurity. Most people become negative about a particular thing because they secretly feel that they cannot change their current state. There is a way to help people overcome their insecurities. People will usually respond very defensively when you begin to touch and address those sensitive areas of self-doubt. Consequently, strong words of encouragement and affirmation are the antidote to counteract the potency of a negative self-image. By showing loving support, you will help them to begin lowering their defenses so that they can be free to begin the journey toward better emotional well being and self-assurance.

When God blesses others the way I want Him to bless me, I'll not become envious. I'll simply get in line! I AM NEXT IN LINE FOR A BLESSING.

> **Gene 26:12** (NIV) Isaac planted crops in that land and the same year reaped a hundredfold, because the LORD blessed him.
>
> **13** The man became rich, and his wealth continued to grow until he became very wealthy.
>
> **14** He had so many flocks and herds and servants that the Philistines envied him.
>
> **15** So all the wells that his father's servants had dug in the time of his father

The Dynamic Points of Optimism

Abraham, the Philistines stopped up, filling them with earth.

Negative people are afraid of becoming positive because it means coming face to face with their internal struggles. We all have to fight the tendency to be negative. Unfortunately, some people love to view the world through a prism of pessimism. A person will expend a great deal of energy, miss out on invaluable sleep, and nearly go crazy fixating on negative and jealous thoughts of others. When, in fact, there is nothing to be jealous about.

> **Pearl of Wisdom**
>
> "True optimism is not forcing a smile in order to convince others that all is well."

Optimism is expectancy in its most generic form. OPTIMISM is an active, empowering, constructive attitude that creates conditions for success by focusing and acting on possibilities and opportunities. If a person desires to live effectively, he or she will have to root out all self-defeating pessimism and replace it with active enthusiasm. True optimism is not forcing a smile in order to convince others that all is well. This will simply be a surface mask to camouflage your confusion and frustration. Once you fully understand and address the fact that negativity may be the culprit holding you back, you will then experience the liberty to begin living a more productive life.

Christians, pastors, businessmen, athletes, co-workers, dancers, recording artist, actors and actresses, etc. are all vulnerable to the attacks of pessimism. Your greatest vulnerability to the attacks of jealousy and negativity will always stem from the success of someone in your own field of

God wants you Healthy, Wealthy & Full of Life

> **Pearl of Wisdom**
>
> "Self-confidence intermingled with self-worth helps form a healthy self-esteem."

expertise. A person is seldom envious of someone in another field. Christians should be the most positive people on the planet. However, many of us have thrown our hats into that same ring of negativity and pessimism. But in all actuality, this should not be the case amongst the ranks of Christians because we have an active, living faith residing inside of us that constantly reminds us that nothing is impossible to them that believe. What an awesome revelation or internal truth!

> **Pearl of Wisdom**
>
> "If people are to expand their lives, overcome their limitations, and develop a technique for improvement, they will have to detach themselves from who they presently are."

I am now going to expose you to seven **(7) dynamic points** that have helped me to stave off attack from the fiery darts of pessimism, insecurity, and jealousy, which have, at some point or another in my life, tried to preclude me from reaching my goals. And I am certain that these seven points will help you by shedding more light on all your possibilities.

Dynamic Point 1: ESTABLISH YOUR SELF-WORTH

Self-confidence intermingled with self-worth helps form a healthy self-esteem. An individual must establish a sense of worth by recognizing that his or her value is not predicated on possessions or accomplishments, but rather on the fact one has infinite intrinsic value in simply being a human being. As individuals, we all have God-given inalienable rights that should fill us with a profound measure of dignity and self-respect. One of the most powerful things you can do is to build a healthy self-image based on God's word. The second most powerful thing you can do is to destroy it.

Dynamic Point 2: ESTABLISH A PROCESS FOR SELF-IMPROVEMENT

If people are to expand their lives, overcome their limitations, and develop a technique for improvement, they will have to detach themselves from who they presently are. If you are one who procrastinates or struggles with self-discipline, you are sabotaging your own success without realizing it. You can change, however, by recognizing the need to become more disciplined and mentally focused on achieving your goals in life. This can be accomplished by changing your present thought patterns. You must formulate a strategy to replace old and self-defeating data with new and improved information, thus starting you on a new and guaranteed path to victory.

> **Pearl of Wisdom**
> "Procrastination is designed to keep you from starting."

Dynamic Point 3: DESTROY PROCRASTINATION

Procrastination works like the breaks on a car; breaks are designed to slow the vehicle or bring it to a complete stop. Procrastination has the same effect when it comes to us pursuing our destiny. When we allow procrastination to take root in our lives, it will short-circuit the very optimism that serves to fuel every ascent to greatness. Optimism cannot flourish if procrastination is in effect. Therefore,

> **Pearl of Wisdom**
> "Vigilance is the key to focus."

procrastination must be uprooted from your life if you are going to succeed in your endeavors. Procrastination is designed to keep you from starting. What you don't start—you cannot finish. In order to destroy procrastination, write down ten reasons to begin the project business or task at hand. Meditate on those reasons. Without justifiable reasons to the contrary, you will discover the motivation to start.

Dynamic Point 4: BE VIGILANT

Vigilance is the key to focus. It also allows us to be aware of our surroundings in order to prevent negative influences from creeping into our lives. Because opposites do attract, positive and hopeful people will always tend to attract doubters and naysayers. Such is the law of opposite attraction. But vigilance must be used to keep the flame of optimism shining brightly on our dreams and endeavors. If we are not careful, we can allow the toxic waste of negative people to pollute the landscape of dreams, preventing us from charting our course towards the object of our hope. Therefore, remain vigilant so that your optimism can light the way.

Dynamic Point 5: TALK POSITIVE

What you say is so important because out of the abundance of the heart the mouth speaks, so the Bible says. It is a fact that when we speak something, we literally give life to our words.

Pearl of Wisdom

"People don't fail at what they do; they fail at what they try."

Pearl of Wisdom

"The word "try" is always used by people who make half-hearted attempts."

The Dynamic Points of Optimism

Consequently, if you are feeling down or if you feel as though nothing is going your way, refuse to speak your frustration so that what you feel cannot come to fruition. Understand that your feelings are not nearly as important as that assignment you've been sent to this earth to accomplish. Speak with absolute clarity the things you desire to happen in your life so that you can create the very environment most conducive to your success. People who usually say what they want to do and what they want to be, rarely ever do and very seldom ever become. People don't fail at what they do; they fail at what they try. If people will learn to harness their tongues, they will avoid giving life to many of their failures and change the course of their lives for the better. The word "try" is always used by people who make half-hearted attempts.

Dynamic Point 6: CHECK YOUR ATTITUDE

How does one gauge his or her attitude? Attitudes are oriented based on our emotions. They soar or tumble based on our mental state. Make no mistake about it, a soaring attitude is connected to a positive thought life. For example, when you watch a movie, the transmitted information will evoke different emotions such happiness or melancholy, anger or bewilderment, excitement or boredom. Understandably then, our attitudes are triggered in large measure due to the information we take in daily. Therefore, if you want your attitude to soar, take in the kind of information that will enable it to soar with eagles. Understand that what you take in

> **Pearl of Wisdom**
>
> "Optimism without faith is like a frame without a picture."

affects what you come to believe, and what you come to believe determines what you come to feel.

Dynamic Point 7: MAINTAIN YOUR FAITH LEVEL

Is faith essential to optimism? Absolutely yes! Optimism and faith are inextricably linked to each other. Optimism cannot truly work without one having active faith in the ability of God. Optimism without faith is like a frame without a picture. Faith provides the ability to see and move towards a goal in the face of everything that contradicts it. Optimism derives because of your faith, not in spite of it. The Bible speaks of little faith, much faith, strong faith, no faith, and weak faith. All suggest the level of faith in operation. Your best results will come from being strong in faith or having much faith. But understand that all of your results will be determined by the level of your faith and its ability to enable you to see beyond your obstacles. You will remain positive, however, when your faith is anchored in God.

chapter four

Projecting A Strong Self-Image

chapter four

Projecting a Strong Self-Image

"We hold these truths to be self-evident, that all men are created equal; that they are endowed by their Creator with inherent and inalienable rights; that among these, are life, liberty, and the pursuit of happiness;"
—*originally written by Thomas Jefferson 1776*

It is your inalienable right to succeed, not just as an American, but as a person. No person has the right to enslave or hinder someone from succeeding in life or business. Although life does not hold any guarantees, the word of God does. You were created to be creative. We are all unique and empowered with the right to imagine anything and therefore produce it. No other creation holds that certifiable right but humans.

You contain the power to influence your personal image or destroy it. Image is created in us by words, facts, and beliefs. We are motivated to become what we imagine ourselves to be. It is very important that you allow God's construction company to establish the right image in you. We are told that two-thirds of our lifetime

> **Pearl of Wisdom**
>
> "We are motivated to become what we imagine ourselves to be."

Projecting A Strong Self-Image

impressions are made before we are seven years old. Most of life's basic knowledge, such as the ability to read and write, is given to us before we are ten years of age. It is this reason that college aptitude tests can be given to children younger than 13 years of age and they still yield amazing results. The formative years of our lives hint at and reveal a wealth of information regarding our purpose here on earth. Likewise, many of our adult problems, more often than not, stem from unresolved issues of childhood. What happened to us in our early years created unhealthy images that caused anxiety, stress, and tension later in our lives. The pain of childhood leaves most people unwilling to revisit those distressing feelings and emotions. As a result, the positive change we desire to occur in our lives cannot take place because unhealthy self-images dominate our mental landscape. In reality, we cannot project a healthy image without first getting rid of unhealthy mental photographs. Every image created has the potential to produce good or evil; success or failure; obedience or disobedience; pride or humility.

An effective method that many professional counselors employ to help their clients deal with emotionally disturbing pasts is to help them tear down old images that have been shaped by negative experiences so that they can be replaced by newer, healthier ones. The greatest fear that most people have is to experience failure in life. Most people experience failure on a consistent basis because of their fear of it. The biblical character Job experienced the power of what fear will produce when we choose to fixate on it.

Job 3:25 (KJS) For the thing which I greatly feared is come upon me, and that which I was afraid of is come unto me.

Aristotle said, "We are what we repeatedly do.

Many of us fail miserably in our personal lives because of what we imagine ourselves to be. More importantly, we allow people to construct in us the image that they perceive us to be, thus, renouncing God's image in us.

> **Pearl of Wisdom**
> "Your personal image is who you perceive yourself to be."

Man's image of himself was stolen in the Garden of Eden when Adam and Eve disobeyed God, and ever since that dreadful day, man has spent a great deal of time hiding from God and also from himself. As a result, it becomes virtually impossible to discover who you are without first discovering God. Once you establish your identity, you will also discover the purpose of your existence.

> **Pearl of Wisdom**
> "Therefore, we are not creatures of circumstance; we are creators of circumstances."

You are here on this planet for a reason. Every created thing has purpose and an assignment here on earth. Your assignment is not decided by you, but rather discovered by you. Your personal image is who you perceive yourself to be. Most people define who they are by what they do, where they are from, or by associations they have with organizations or other people. The problem many people have is trying to live up to the perceptions of others. When this occurs over a long period of time, people have difficulty locating their true identities.

Projecting A Strong Self-Image

It reminds me of individuals who are called by their nick names for so long that they fail to respond to their given names.

As beings created in God's image, we have the right to be creative. Therefore, we are not creatures of circumstance; we are creators of circumstances. You have the solution to every problem that you may confront in life.

> "We are all creative, but by the time we are three or four years old, someone has knocked the creativity out of us. Some people shut up the kids who start to tell stories. Kids dance in their cribs, but someone will insist they sit still. By the time the creative people are ten or twelve, they want to be like everyone else."
> *–Maya Angelo*

I one day asked my son if he intends to be successful when he gets older. His reply was an emphatic, "I know that I am going to make it!" How do you know? I asked, "Because God didn't give me this talent to fail."

The man who follows the crowd will usually get no further than the crowd. The man who walks alone is likely to find himself in places no one has ever been. What you cannot do is what you believe is impossible for you. Don't become angry with the one who performs what you believed you could not do. Your gifts are not gifts as long as you keep them to yourself. They are given to you to give to

Pearl of Wisdom

"If your self-image changes as a result of what someone says about you, good, bad or indifferent, you don't have a self-image; you have a people image."

someone else. The unfortunate thing is that we sale our gifts in order to get money instead of money coming as a result of our gifts.

> **Pearl of Wisdom**
>
> "Choose your friends very carefully, because they may very well be your enemies."

If your self-image changes as a result of what someone says about you, good, bad or indifferent, you don't have a self-image; you have a people image. You may not want to admit this, but your lack of self-esteem is fed to you from people whom you admire. Understand, however, they may not admire you. They may attempt to marginalize you as an individual by insisting that God only blessed you because of them. When in reality, God may have only blessed them because of you. As long as you keep people like this around you, you will never succeed.

> **Pearl of Wisdom**
>
> "The worst aspect of the 'negative self concept' is that once you start seeing yourself as a failure, you begin to act the part."

Choose your friends very carefully, because they may very well be your enemies. Jesus trained 12 men to be His disciples; one betrayed Him, one denied Him, and another one doubted Him. Only one, John, was with Him during His suffering and crucifixion. While 11 disciples thought that Jesus was at the lowest point in His three-year ministry, John was the only one to get a glimpse of Him at the apex of His earthly ministry, which was while He hung on the cross.

The way you see yourself affects not only your thoughts, but how others perceive you. If you possess a negative self-image, you will project it outwardly to the world. The worst aspect of the 'negative self concept' is that once you start seeing yourself as a failure, you begin to act the part.

Negative feelings feed on themselves and become a vicious, growing cycle which can encompass all your thoughts, actions and relationships. The great thing is that no matter how badly you've been treated and how little self-esteem you have, it is possible to change the way you see yourself.

The first step in the journey towards a greater self-worth is self-knowledge. The more realistic and accurate your self-concept, the greater the value it will have for you. Your self-esteem can be improved by reducing the gap between that **'ideal self'** which is what you and others imagine you to be and the 'actual self' which is what God created you to be. The shorter the distance between your ideal self and your real self, the higher the level of your self-esteem and the closer you are to the Kingdom of God."

God wants you Healthy, Wealthy & Full of Life

chapter five

Discovering the Wealth Within

chapter five

Discovering the Wealth Within

> **Pearl of Wisdom**
>
> "People can have a wealth of ability, but if they do not recognize their ability they will never tap into their wealth."

People can have a wealth of ability, but if they do not recognize their ability they will never tap into their wealth. Wealth does not seek out the wisest, the strongest, or the most intelligent; it waits for those qualities to seek it out. 4.6% of America's households have a net worth of one million or more. 48% of that percentage is white, 18% is Black and 16% is Hispanic. Wealth in our free enterprise system is there for the taking. Money has no racial propensities or biases. Whoever values money, will value its use. **No dreams, no realities!**

> **Pearl of Wisdom**
>
> "Whoever values money, will value its use."

On day two of a recent business meeting I conducted, a lady approached me after hearing me speak and stated "Mr. Brown, I can't sleep." Out of concern, I asked, "What is the matter." She said, "I have all these thoughts of various businesses I can start." It's great that you have thoughts about businesses that you can start, but what are you going to do about the thoughts? Usually, people get stuck right about here because they are bombarded with ideas that can potentially create a great deal of money, but they don't have a clue as to how to get the ideas from their heads onto the assembly line. Take the following test to assess your creative potential. Take a blank sheet of white paper and stare at it for a couple of minutes and then write something on it. If what you put on the paper doesn't make sense, do it again until it makes sense (cents). If you put nothing on the paper, you need to continue working for someone else until you can complete this exercise. This exercise will expose the potential for putting your dreams into action. No dreams, no realities.

There are 4 questions you need to ask yourself before you buy a home(s), start a business, or invest in stocks and bonds. I have asked myself these four questions time and time again throughout my life, and I have thought long and hard about my personal answers, as you must yourselves. It is important that you understand exactly where you are spiritually and mentally concerning the issue of money.

Why strive for excellence when mediocrity is perfectly acceptable by most people's standards? People, your vision of where you want to go and who you want to become is the greatest gauge of your achievement and the most powerful built-in navigational system you have. Without a goal it is difficult to keep score. Don't seek praise, seek constructive criticism. Those you trust to give you truthful answers can help you whether you like their criticism or not. Constructive criticism from a person with character will help you eliminate the flaws in your gameplan.

Pearl of Wisdom
"No dreams, no realities."

Pearl of Wisdom
"Without a goal it is difficult to keep score."

Pearl of Wisdom
"Don't seek praise, seek constructive criticism."

So, what are these four questions and why are they so significant? Be patient; I'll soon reveal all four questions. After hearing the questions and answering them correctly, they will become strategic pillars to help you while on your journey toward success. Some people have made the claim that they were already a success. My questions then are, "In what area of life are you a success, and when did you reach your destination?"

Success is described by the following words: degree or measure of succeeding favorable or desired outcome; in conjunction to the attainment of wealth, favor, or eminence, one that succeeds

The template for success is already laid out in your bible—you just have to read it, know it, believe it and do it. **It will profit you nothing to know it and not apply it.**

> **Josh 1:7 (NIV)** Be strong and very courageous. Be careful to obey all the law my servant Moses gave you; do not turn from it to the right or to the left **(don't allow anything to cause you to digress)**, that you may be successful wherever you go.
> 8 Do not let this Book of the Law depart from your mouth; meditate on it day and night, so that you may be careful to do everything written in it. Then you will be prosperous and successful. **KJV** "thou shalt make (compose, create, invent, arrange) thy way prosperous, and then thou shalt have good success."

9 Have I not commanded you? Be strong and courageous. Do not be terrified; do not be discouraged, for the LORD your God will be with you wherever you go."
10 So Joshua ordered the officers of the people:
11 "Go through the camp and tell the people, `Get your supplies ready. Three days from now you will cross the Jordan here to go in and take possession of the land the LORD your God is giving you for your own.'"

Here are the four questions that you should seriously consider:
1. Do you believe that God wants you wealthy, healthy, and full of life?
2. Will you risk everything you own on God's promises for you?
3. Do you believe that God alone decides how much wealth you acquire in life?
4. Why do you want to become wealthy, and do you have a plan to succeed?

Eccl 3:12 (TLB) So I conclude that, first, there is nothing better for a man than to be happy and to enjoy himself as long as he can;
13 and second, that he should eat and drink and enjoy the fruits of his labors, for these are gifts from God.
14 And I know this, that whatever God does is final--nothing can be added or

taken from it; God's purpose in this is that man should fear the all-powerful God.

Isaac, the son of Abraham, experienced two levels of wealth—rich and very wealthy. Most Christians are simply trying to achieve the first. And many of them settle for the empty promises of get-rich-quick pyramid schemes and overnight-wealth, multi-level marketing plans. Please don't misunderstand me; I'm not knocking those concepts. Many people have made very good money through multi-level marketing ventures. On the other hand, 4 to 5 times as many people will never prosper financially as these programs promise.

> **Gene 26:12 (NIV)** Isaac planted crops in that land and the same year reaped a hundredfold, because the LORD blessed him.
> **13** The man became rich, and his wealth continued to grow until he became very wealthy.
> **14** He had so many flocks and herds and servants that the Philistines envied him.

How did Isaac become rich? Answer the question please! Allow me to repeat the question! How did Isaac become rich? Most people will read this passage and conclude that God, by supernatural means, somehow made Isaac rich. The scripture does not say this. The normal response is "God made Isaac rich" because we take comfort in being able to put the responsibility on God for how much or how little money we make. Moreover, fixing responsibility with God absolves us of any responsibility where our financial conditions are concerned.

"Isaac planted" is the key to his success. God cannot bless what you refuse to do. Isaac had to put his ability to work in order to see results in his life. Please note that God blessed Isaac. When you are blessed, everything you do will prosper. Every seed has the potential to produce more than a single crop. This was not a supernatural blessing. God simply allowed the elements to help produce a maximum harvest.

My next question is how did Isaac become very wealthy? Please read the scripture very carefully. As humans, we have the tendency to not see things as they truly are, but how we perceive them to be while looking through the lens of our present emotional, intellectual, and spiritual conditions. The answer is simple. His wealth continued to grow, and as a result, he became very wealthy. From Isaac's example, we are able to conclude that we play a major role in determining the size and extent of our wealth, not God. We determine whether we become simply "rich" or "rich and very wealthy." When a person becomes very wealthy, he simply acquires more of what he already had.

How did Isaac get more? What you don't see in the previous verse is what he had to do in order to have more. Obviously, Isaac had to continue planting and feeding his flocks, but he also had to trade and negotiate in order to produce more. If the scripture says that God blessed Isaac, God had to give him

God wants you Healthy, Wealthy & Full of Life

the knowledge and ability to become successful in his line of work.

Let's face it. In this world, we <u>all</u> need money. I am certain that you already know beyond a shadow of any doubt that you have the ability to acquire a certain level of wealth the evidence is in what you have earned in the past and in what you are currently amassing. But you may struggle with whether you have the wherewithal to punch through that glass ceiling to tap into the "rich and very wealthy" blessings that exist at the next level.

In many respects, the errant teachings that pervade widely throughout the Church on this particular topic have contributed directly to the reason why so many of God's people struggle when it comes to building wealth. Your perspective of money is determined by your baseline level of understanding. How much of it you acquire in a lifetime is conditioned based on how high you set your ceiling and also on how much faith you employ to scale those heights to possess it. Understand that all the money you will ever want or need is already inside of you.

Oftentimes we think that we are being unspiritual, selfish, greedy, ungodly, or flat out sinful if we voice our desire to have money. Money is not a sin; and neither is owning an abundance of it.

> **1 Tim 6:10 (NIV)** For the **love of money** is a **root** (*cause*) of all kinds of evil. Some people, eager for money, have wandered from the faith and pierced themselves with

> **Pearl of Wisdom**
>
> "The tangible derives from the intangible and the visible is branded by the invisible."

many griefs.

The majority of this world's population is money illiterate. We all need more education in the area of financial management, but many people deny the existence of a need for growth in this area. Furthermore, most people feel very uncomfortable expressing a strong desire to become abundantly wealthy. The first lesson that we should be willing to learn is "how to master the basic principles that govern money." This understanding will lead many to financial freedom. Your ability to exercise your faith to get it, invest it, use it, spend it, and manage it is a powerful witness to those who may struggle in this area.

Most people are not profitable because they simply do not know how to profit. The spiritual precedes the mental and the mental precedes the natural. The tangible derives from the intangible and the visible is branded by the invisible. Every tangible thing on earth owes its existence to a single thought whether spoken into existence by God or invented into being by man.

When a person performs what he or she believes, it is an **EX**ternal proof of an **IN**ternal faith! When you sow your seeds (money) into God's work, your offering is evident that you have what you offered it for. Money represents you! It is your time, your sweat, your energy, your mental abilities—thus a major part of you. It is the POWER part of your life. When you give to God's work, it is an **EX**pression of your **IM**pression. Remember that your car, your home, your business, your children, your financial status and your clothes are an expression of your impression about you.

chapter six

Mastering the Fundamentals of Success

chapter six

Mastering The Fundamentals of Success

"I hated every minute of training, but I said, 'Don't quit. Suffer now and live the rest of your life as a champion.''
—*Muhammad Ali*

I am a firm believer that success is not an accident. Unlike the millions of Americans that play the lottery in hopes that they will one day buy the winning ticket—I believe that I am the winning ticket. Aristotle said, "Excellence is not an act, but a habit." Your future success will rise or fall based on your willingness to submit to properly train. Every winner in life has one common trait; they have learned to master the fundamentals of success.

Michael Jordan in my personal opinion is arguably the greatest NBA player to ever play the game of basketball. It was often said by many of Michael's college and NBA teammates that he was usually the first one on the court and the last one to leave. Michael Jordan became great because he mastered the fundamentals of basketball. He was not just known for his ability to shoot jump shots, but free

> **Pearl of Wisdom**
>
> "Every winner in life has one common trait; they have learned to master the fundamentals of success."

God wants you Healthy, Wealthy & Full of Life

> **Pearl of Wisdom**
>
> "The success of your income has already been predetermined by your initial labor input."

a test was flunked by a student, you better believe that those failures can be traced back to either refusing to listen to sound counsel or that the person chose to listen to the wrong voice. The success of your income has already been predetermined by your initial labor input. What you put into your training will be far greater in its return. The return is always greater than your initial investment, and the accolades will always far exceed your training.

Mastering the Fundamentals of Success

throws, slam dunks, lay ups, and he was an excellent defensive player. When the NBA players went to play in the 2004 Olympics, it was for certain that they would win the gold. In fact, many in the United States did not expect anything less than a gold metal. But as they played, we became painfully aware that these guys had great jumping ability, excellent dribbling skills, and some of the best coaches in the NBA; but they had not mastered the fundamentals.

Everything in life has an origin or principle that governs the success in a particular area. Meaning, you will not succeed if you have not learned the system or rules of engagement in your field of interest. Life itself has rules. Rules are the governing factor of everything on planet earth; and how well you learn and submit to those rules will determine the level of your success.

Mastering the fundamentals of success is imperative if you are going to move beyond your base level. It's similar to trying to pass a Trigonometry or Calculus test without understanding basic arithmetic. You know as well as I do that that will never happen. Your capacity to achieve success in a certain area has already been predetermined by your willingness to listen to the kind of words that will instruct you on how to succeed. Your readiness to prepare and to be coached or mentored is evident of your passion and desire to succeed. You cannot escape this fundamental principle of success.

When a business fails or a marriage is torn apart, or

Pearl of Wisdom

"Mastering the fundamentals of success is imperative if you are going to move beyond your base level."

Reaching for the Top

chapter seven

Reaching for the Top

I believe that one of the greatest lies told to religious people and a good percentage of the American public today is that it is prideful and sinful to desire more money and to have a greater position in life. If having a desire to have more money is a sin, then everyone on the planet lives in a state of hopelessness. Preachers have instructed us to be happy with the job we presently have and our barely over minimum wage salary. Most people are genetically predisposed to poverty or living under a mountain of debt because we are being taught to live in this manner. This is the key cause to why so many Christians have problems with success or being successful. Preachers have placed the pie in the sky and the hell on earth syndrome into the psyche of their parishioners. Sunday morning messages are inundated with encouraging messages that life's problems will soon be over when you get to heaven, leaving no remedy for living victorious and successful lives on earth.

Most people don't pursue and reach for the top because it is less tempting to settle for things at the

Reaching for the Top

bottom. Not only do people want to have the money but many of them need to make more money. Wouldn't you like to take your family on that much needed vacation or to be able to buy the kind of clothing that doesn't lose its body after the first washing? Inwardly these people would like to have more, but outwardly they despise those who have what they only dreamed of having. Ignorance is the only true enemy capable of destroying a person. People that do not succeed in life are simply living a self-defeating lifestyle. God has guaranteed your success in this life and He only requires that we conduct our lives in concert with His principles.

In my book *"Beyond Ordinary,"* I wrote about a man who supervised a plant, and he informed me of his concerns of some of the job applicants. "All the competition for jobs in our plant is at the bottom. Ninety-eight percent of the applications that come across my desk are for an assembly line worker." he exclaimed. If you find yourself always settling for mediocre position, you are in no position to criticize the wealthy. The power to reach for the top resides in you. There is always little or no room at the bottom because it is the comfort zone for most people. People that will wait at the bottom of a fruit tree usually don't mine eating rotten fruit. A person stoops for the bottom, but reaches for the top.

> **Pearl of Wisdom**
> "People that do not succeed in life are simply living a self-defeating lifestyle."

> **Pearl of Wisdom**
> "There is always little or no room at the bottom because it is the comfort zone for most people."

God wants you Healthy, Wealthy & Full of Life

chaptereight

I Can...

chapter eight

I Can...

> **Pearl of Wisdom**
>
> "The mouth will never operate without consent from the mind."

It has been said that the rational mind is a wonderful servant but a terrible master. We must control the mind instead of giving it free reign to run wild. If we do not control the mind, it will solicit the aid of the mouth and the tongue, and together they will lead us into big trouble. If you tackle the virtually uncontrollable tongue, it will be because you have learned to harness your thinking. The mouth will never operate without consent from the mind.

A man was troubled with dizzy spells and he went from one doctor to another, but none could diagnose the problem. He began to lose weight, and stopped sleeping at night. His health continued to deteriorate to the point that he began to prepare for the worst...

He picked out a suit, shoes, socks, and asked the for a size 15 shirt. The store clerk said, "Sir, you need between a 16-17 size shirt. But the man insisted that he wore a size 15. Finally, in exasperation, the clerk said, "But if you wear a size fifteen you'll get dizzy spells."

The most difficult part of helping a person to change is getting them to want to change their crippling mentality. A mind that is not harnessed will produce and justify failure, destroy relationships, conjure ill feelings, and rationalize the destruction of its own body. I have learned that the body can change if the person is willing to change their thinking pattern. It is neither your body nor your mouth which is usually out of control; it is your mind that is out of control.

> "If you can control a man's thinking, you do not have to worry about his action. When you determine what a man shall think you do not have to concern yourself about what he will do. If you make a man feel that he is inferior, you do not have to compel him to accept an inferior status, for he will seek it himself. If you make a man think that he is justly an outcast; you do not have to order him to the back door. He will go without being told; and if there is no back door, his very nature will demand one."
>
> —*Carter G. Woodson*

It has been said by Edward Louis Cole, "Sow an action and you will reap a habit; sow a habit and you will reap a character; sow a character and you will reap a destiny." How you think about life will determine all the activities of your life. Habits are determined by your actions. Habits are things that

Pearl of Wisdom

"Habits are determined by your actions."

you practice without realizing. The proof of your dedication to your dream is your willingness to deliberately develop good habits that are conducive to your success.

Jesus spent three years of earthly ministry raising the level of thinking in those who followed Him. Everything Jesus did was His way of demonstrating to us that we can do it, too.

> Two weekend fishermen were in a boat fishing. One man caught three large trout and threw them back into the water. Whenever he caught smaller fish, he would keep them. The other fisherman puzzled by his actions asked, "Why are you throwing back the large fish and keeping the fish that are no bigger than a small sardine?" "My frying pan is small," replied the man.

This man turned down opportunities because he was restricted by the size of his frying pan. How many wealth-creating opportunities have you thrown back because you believed your capacity was limited? Don't fear success because it is God's design for your life. Whenever you're stretched, your capacity is enlarged. The law of wealth could care less about who you are, what your background is, or your race or gender. It will simply yield its way to those who have learned to apply its principles.

Roma 12:2 (NIV) Do not conform any longer to the pattern of this world, but be

---

Pearl of Wisdom

"Don't fear success because it is God's design for your life."

transformed by the renewing of your mind. Then you will be able to test and approve what God's will is--his good, pleasing and perfect will.
3 For by the grace given me I say to every one of you: Do not think of yourself more highly than you ought, but rather think of yourself with sober judgment, in accordance with the measure of faith God has given you.

People that usually wrestle with low self-esteem do not have a good God-esteem. Building your worth-value is discovering what God says about you. A handicapped man was recorded saying, "I know I'm going to make it in spite of my handicap. I refuse to be a prisoner of a wheel chair. I know I can make it."

If I can get the pessimist to say that they can do something, we can eliminate, if not all, most of the negativity in the world today. There are not enough of people saying, "I can do all things!" We can be at least ten times more powerful, at least ten times more-happier and freer and stronger than what we already are. We can be ten times more active, more alive, more spiritual, more faithful, and more Godlike if we will only say, "I Can!"

> **Phil 4:13 (KJS)** I can do all things through Christ which strengtheneth me.

You can elevate superior to every condition in your life through the strength that Christ gives. It's not

Pearl of Wisdom

"We can be ten times more active, more alive, more spiritual, more faithful, and more Godlike if we will only say, "I Can!"

Pearl of Wisdom

"It's not the load that breaks you down, it's the way you have been taught to carry it."

God wants you Healthy, Wealthy & Full of Life

Pearl of Wisdom

"The solution to all of your problems is concealed in "I Can't."

the load that breaks you down, it's the way you have been taught to carry it. Limitations are a learned behavior pattern that causes people to under achieve in spite of their ability to over achieve. Our minds must be conditioned to tackle the tough and difficult tasks, but it must not be allowed to develop an image that these objectives are too much to overcome. Or else our creative juices will dry up and we will not be able to innovate new ways to do a particular thing.

> An overburdened and overworked ant was carrying a piece of straw across a large slab of concrete. The straw was so long and heavy that the tiny insect staggered beneath its weight. Nonetheless, the ant was committed to completing its task. Finally, as the stress of its burden began to take its toll, the little ant was brought to a halt by a gaping crack in its path. The ant saw no way of getting across or around the deep divide. Then a thought suddenly struck. Carefully laying the straw across the gulf, the ant walked over it and safely reached the other side. The ant's heavy load had become a helpful bridge because he was committed to his task.

The solution to all of your problems is concealed in "I Can't." If you believe that you cannot achieve your objective, whatever the case may be, your mental system will shut down and the answers to life's problems will remain hidden. The words "I Can" will expose you to opportunities that were there all along. These two powerful words are not magical words that will give you supernatural strength; they are simply words that will propel you to perform what you were always capable of doing.

God wants you Healthy, Wealthy & Full of Life

Pearls of Wisdom

CHAPTER 1
The Principle of Being Healthy, Wealthy, And Full of Life

- "When you relax the standard, you lessen the quality"

- "Excuses are tools of incompetence that lead people down the path of failure that they will eventually adapt to and embrace as part of their lifestyle."

- "People who have amassed great wealth believe they're entitled to it, while those without much wealth hold negative views of those who possess it."

- "What you believe about wealth and money is directly proportionate to how much of it you possess."

- "God is not the God of just enough; He is the God of more than enough."

- "How much is too much?"

- "The more you are exposed to truth, the clearer your directions will be in life."

- "Lack is not an option when abundance is a lifestyle."

- "A healthy person can enjoy his or her wealth."

- "When men have run out of options, God becomes the only option."

CHAPTER 2
You Were Born to Be Great

- "People with fame have a job to perform, but people with greatness have a calling to answer."

- "Intimidation is birthed out of the sphere of comparisons."

- "Mediocrity is the kryptonite to greatness."

- "Greatness does not make you perfect; it exposes your willingness to pursue it."

- "There are winners and there are losers; and there are people who would like to think that they are somewhere in the middle."

CHAPTER 3
The Dynamic Points of Optimism

- " If there is anybody who needs to be convinced about your ability to succeed—it is you!"

- "When we choose to use others as the yardstick to measure our success, we will always fall prey to destructive feelings of insecurity."

- "True optimism is not forcing a smile in order to convince others that all is well."

- "Self-confidence intermingled with self-worth helps form a healthy self-esteem."

- "If people are to expand their lives, overcome their limitations, and develop a technique for improvement, they will have to detach themselves from who they presently are."

- "Procrastination is designed to keep you from starting."

- "Vigilance is the key to focus."

- "People don't fail at what they do; they fail at what they try."

- "The word "try" is always used by people who make half-hearted attempts."

- "Optimism without faith is like a frame without a picture."

CHAPTER 4
Projecting a Strong Self-Image

- "We are motivated to become what we imagine ourselves to be."

- "Your personal image is who you perceive yourself to be."

- "Therefore, we are not creatures of circumstance; we are creators of circumstances."

- "If your self-image changes as a result of what someone says about you, good, bad or indifferent, you don't have a self-image; you have a people image."

- "Choose your friends very carefully, because they may very well be your enemies."

- "The worst aspect of the 'negative self concept' is that once you start seeing yourself as a failure, you begin to act the part."

CHAPTER 5
Discovering the Wealth Within

- "People can have a wealth of ability, but if they do not recognize their ability they will never tap into their wealth."

- "Whoever values money, will value its use."

- "No dreams, no realities."

- "Without a goal it is difficult to keep score."

- "Don't seek praise, seek constructive criticism."

- "The tangible derives from the intangible and the visible is branded by the invisible."

CHAPTER 6
Mastering the Fundamentals of Success

- "Every winner in life has one common trait; they have learned to master the fundamentals of success."

- "Mastering the fundamentals of success is imperative if you are going to move beyond your base level."

- "The success of your income has already been predetermined by your initial labor input."

CHAPTER 7
Reaching for the Top

- "People that do not succeed in life are simply living a self-defeating lifestyle."

- "There is always little or no room at the bottom because it is the comfort zone for most people."

CHAPTER 8
I Can...

- "The mouth will never operate without consent from the mind."

- "Habits are determined by your actions."

- "Don't fear success because it is God's design for your life."

- "We can be ten times more active, more alive, more spiritual, more faithful, and more Godlike if we will only say, "I Can!"

- "It's not the load that breaks you down, it's the way you have been taught to carry it."

- "The solution to all of your problems is concealed in "I Can't.""

"Power" Notes

"Power" Notes

"Power" Notes

About the Author

Dr. Mikel Brown is an author, businessman, and religious leader who resides in El Paso, Texas with his wife and two children. He is the President and CEO of CJC Enterprises and owner and CEO of Power Communications Network, through which he conducts seminars and special events. His much sought after style of communicating and humor has made him a favorite for business conclaves and church conventions.

Brian Tracy

Best Selling Author, Entrepreneur, & Success Expert

said this about...

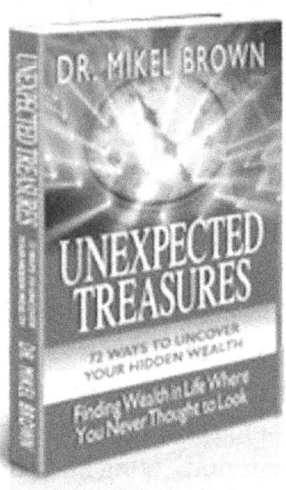

"This book shows you how to develop optimism, resilience, and persistence no matter what happens to you. **It can change your life!**"

Order Your Copy Today!

Scan w/ Your Smart Phone

Available at These Fine Book Retailers

amazon

BARNES & NOBLE

BAM! BOOKS·A·MILLION

or order at www.MikelBrown.com/UT

Don't Continue Wishing You Had More Money

Discover How You Can Easily Start A
Multi-Million Dollar Company
With Less than $100!

*This is NOT a MLM Program

 Use #BWFTGU to add your thoughts to the discussion.

Order Your Copy Today!

Scan w/ Your
Smart Phone

Available at These Fine Book Retailers

or order at www.MikelBrown.com/BW

Get Connected With Dr. Mikel Brown

Websites

www.HowToFixYourMarriage.com
www.DreamMakers99.com
www.MikelBrown.com

Books

Videos

**FREE
e-book offer**

*You Can Think
Your Way To Success*

Get It Today at
www.MikelBrown.com

 /DrMikelBrown   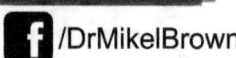 /DrMikelBrown    /DrMikelBrown

www.ingramcontent.com/pod-product-compliance
Lightning Source LLC
Chambersburg PA
CBHW052110070526
44584CB00017B/2413